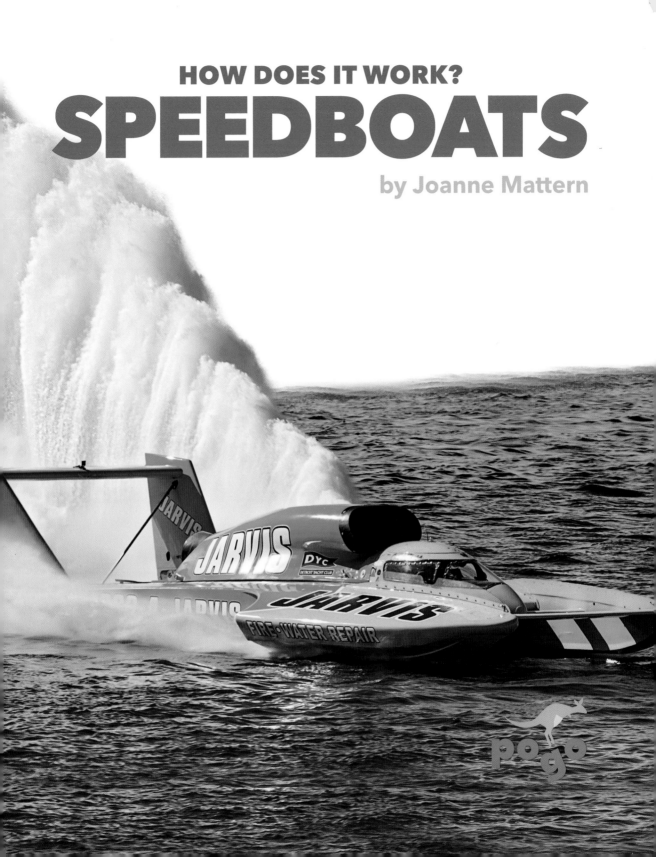

HOW DOES IT WORK?
SPEEDBOATS

by Joanne Mattern

pogo

Ideas for Parents and Teachers

Pogo Books let children practice reading informational text while introducing them to nonfiction features such as headings, labels, sidebars, maps, and diagrams, as well as a table of contents, glossary, and index.

Carefully leveled text with a strong photo match offers early fluent readers the support they need to succeed.

Before Reading

- "Walk" through the book and point out the various nonfiction features. Ask the student what purpose each feature serves.
- Look at the glossary together. Read and discuss the words.

Read the Book

- Have the child read the book independently.
- Invite him or her to list questions that arise from reading.

After Reading

- Discuss the child's questions. Talk about how he or she might find answers to those questions.
- Prompt the child to think more. Ask: What did you know about speedboats before you read this book? What more do you want to learn after reading it?

Pogo Books are published by Jump!
5357 Penn Avenue South
Minneapolis, MN 55419
www.jumplibrary.com

Library of Congress Cataloging-in-Publication Data

Names: Mattern, Joanne, 1963- author.
Title: Speedboats / by Joanne Mattern.
Description: Minneapolis, MN : Jump!, Inc., [2018]
Series: How does it work? | Audience: Ages 7-10.
Includes bibliographical references and index.
Identifiers: LCCN 2017032876 (print)
LCCN 2017032409 (ebook) | ISBN 9781624966996 (ebook) | ISBN 9781620319109 (hardcover : alk. paper)
ISBN 9781620319116 (pbk.)
Subjects: LCSH: Motorboats—Juvenile literature. Boats and boating—Juvenile literature.
Classification: LCC VM341 (print) | LCC VM341 .M377 2017 (ebook) | DDC 623.82/31—dc23
LC record available at https://lccn.loc.gov/2017032876

Editor: Jenna Trnka
Book Designer: Leah Sanders
Photo Researcher: Leah Sanders

Photo Credits: Steve Sparrow/Getty, cover; Darren Brode/Shutterstock, 1, 16; Yevhenii Chulovskyi/Shutterstock, 3; Pedro Monteiro/Shutterstock, 4; Vira Mylyan-Monastyrska/Shutterstock, 5; Equatore/Adobe Stock, 6-7; DoublePHOTO studio/Shutterstock, 8-9; Chuck Wagner/Shutterstock, 10; Kaminskiy/Shutterstock, 11; Kelvin Murray/Getty, 12-13; Warren Little/Getty, 14-15; Matthew Faul/Alamy, 17; Francois Nel/Getty, 18-19; Jenyateua/iStock, 20-21; aabeele/Shutterstock, 23.

Printed in the United States of America at Corporate Graphics in North Mankato, Minnesota.

TABLE OF CONTENTS

CHAPTER 1

HOW IT WORKS

Splash! Zoom! A boat zips past. But it is not an ordinary boat. It speeds and skips across the water. It is a speedboat!

Speedboats are amazing machines. How does a speedboat work? Let's find out!

Speedboats have powerful **motors**. Motors burn gasoline. This creates **energy**. That energy makes speedboats go fast! Some big speedboats have more than one motor. The more motors a boat has, the faster it can go.

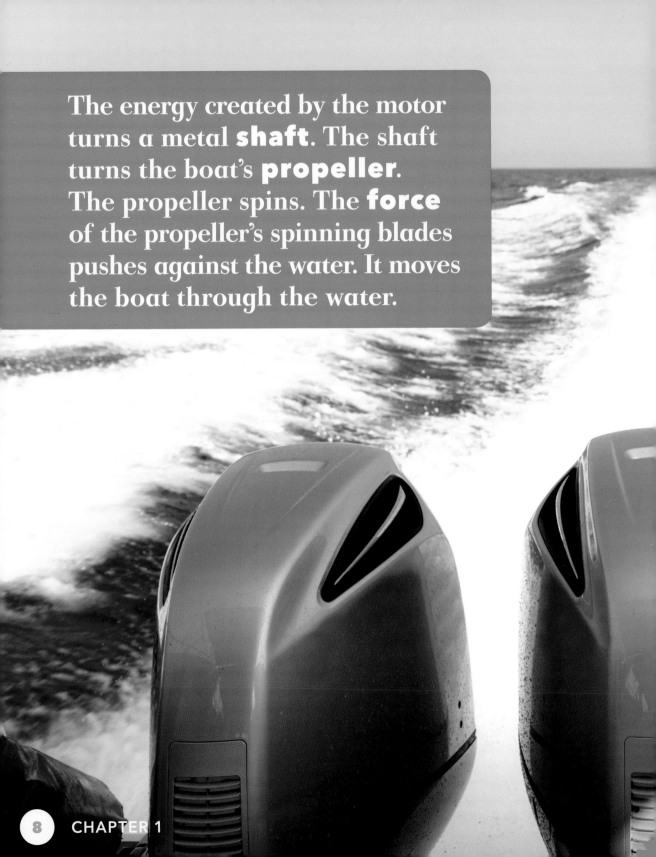

The energy created by the motor turns a metal **shaft**. The shaft turns the boat's **propeller**. The propeller spins. The **force** of the propeller's spinning blades pushes against the water. It moves the boat through the water.

TAKE A LOOK!

A speedboat has many parts that make it go.

MOTOR

STEERING WHEEL

PROPELLER

HULL

CHAPTER 2

BOATS FLOAT

A boat's shape also helps it move through the water. A speedboat **hull** is long and flat. The front of the boat is pointed. It parts the water.

hull

UCAS OIL
SilverHook 48GP

77

The pointed shape creates less **resistance** from the water. This helps the boat cut through the water and gain more **speed**.

Boats are made to float. Boats float because their hulls hold a lot of air. The air makes the boat less **dense** than the water. This allows the boat to float on the water's surface.

DID YOU KNOW?

Many speedboat hulls are made of **fiberglass**. Fiberglass is stronger than steel. It won't bend, scratch, or burn.

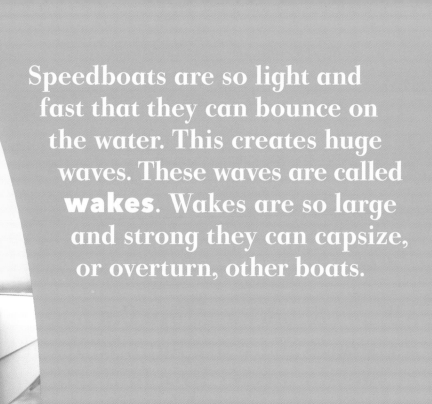

Speedboats are so light and fast that they can bounce on the water. This creates huge waves. These waves are called **wakes**. Wakes are so large and strong they can capsize, or overturn, other boats.

CHAPTER 3

DIFFERENT KINDS OF SPEEDBOATS

All speedboats are fast. But not all look the same. There are many different kinds of speedboats. Hydroplanes look like airplanes. They **skim** over the surface of the water.

A catamaran has two hulls. These boats are light and fast. Powerboats and v-boats have one hull.

powerboat

catamaran

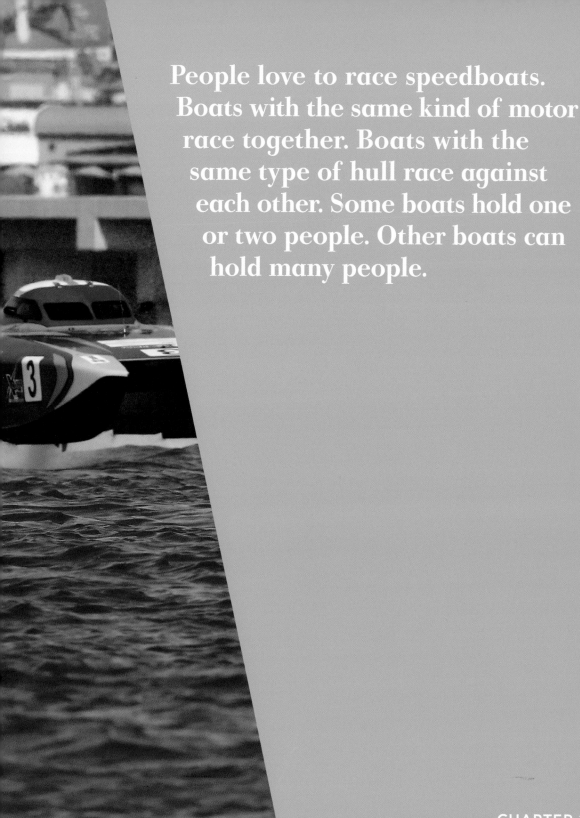

People love to race speedboats. Boats with the same kind of motor race together. Boats with the same type of hull race against each other. Some boats hold one or two people. Other boats can hold many people.

People are always looking for new shapes and power to make speedboats faster. Zoom! The speedboat races away. Look how fast it can go!

O-FUTURO.EU
23
FAMILY
HYDRO GP
HENCZ RÓBERT
CNC
CIRCOLO NAUTICO CHIAVENNA

ACTIVITIES & TOOLS

FLOAT YOUR OWN BOAT

Shape matters when it comes to floating boats. Shapes that spread out the weight of the boat or that hold air work best. They make the boat less dense so it can float.

What You Need:
- modeling clay
- large plastic bowl
- water
- towel

❶ **Fill the bowl with water.**

❷ **Drop a lump of clay into the water. What happens? It sinks. That's because the clay is more dense than the water.**

❸ **Mold the clay into different boat shapes. Test each shape in the water. What shapes float best? What sinks?**

GLOSSARY

dense: How heavy or light an object is for its size.

energy: Power that is used to operate a machine.

fiberglass: A strong material made of thin, flexible glass fibers.

force: Strength or power.

hull: The body of a boat.

motors: Machines, powered either by electricity or gasoline, that power and move a vehicle.

propeller: A device with blades that turn rapidly to move a powerboat.

resistance: Force that opposes the motion of an object.

shaft: A metal rod.

skim: To move quickly across a surface.

speed: The rate at which something moves.

wakes: The waves left in the water by a moving boat.

INDEX

TO LEARN MORE

Learning more is as easy as 1, 2, 3.

1) Go to www.factsurfer.com

2) Enter "speedboats" into the search box.

3) Click the "Surf" button to see a list of websites.

With factsurfer, finding more information is just a click away.